1

2

3

The Lord God Who is Never Too Far Away.

By

John C Burt.

4

Photograph courtesy of
ben - klea
unsplash.com

5

6

1.

FOREWORD :

I want in this very book to think about the concept of the LORD GOD ALMIGHTY being closer to us than we sometimes believe? The

title of this very book is :
" The Lord God Who Is
Never Too Far Away ." My
own belief , is that, the LORD
GOD ALMIGHTY is closer to
us as His people than we
might think at times. If you
are a believer in the Lord
Jesus Christ; then you have
access to the Father through
the Son of God, the Lord
Jesus Christ. Also, you have
the very real gift of the
presence of the Holy Spirit

within you; as a believer in the Lord Jesus Christ. The Holy Spirit; He is the third person of the trinity . So , therefore when we as believer's in the Lord Jesus Christ we can have the third person of the trinity, the Holy Spirit, the Lord God Himself living within ourselves.

All of which is why the book is entitled " The Lord God Who Is Never Too Far Away " . You may believe that because of your failure to obey the Lord

10

God He has suddenly moved
or left you but the Lord Jesus
Christ promised ' to never
leave us or forsake us as
believer's in Him . '   In this
very book I want to take some
time to think about and actively
discuss the LORD GOD
ALMIGHTY who is nearer to
us as believer's than we might
think and believe at different
times in our own lives.

14

2.

Some Scriptural Citations having to do with the topic at hand ; the nearness of the LORD GOD.

16

(N I V)

Exodus 25 : 30.

(30) " Put the bread of the Presence on this table to be before me at all times."

Exodus 33 : 14.

(14) " The LORD replied, " My Presence will go with you, and I will give you rest. "

17

Numbers 4 : 7.

(7) " Over the table
of the Presence they are
to spread a blue cloth and
put on it plates, dishes
and bowls; and the jars
for drink offerings; the
bread that is continually
there is to remain on it. "

! Samuel 6 : 20.

(20) " and the men
of Beth Shemesh a said,

18

" Who can stand in the presence of the LORD, this holy God? To whom will the ark go up from here ? "

2 Kings 23 : 27.

(27) " So the LORD said, " I will remove Judah also from my presence as I removed Israel, and I will reject Jerusalem , the City I chose, and this temple

19

about which I said, " There shall my Name be. "

Psalm 16 : 11.

(11) " You have made known to me the path of life; you will fill me with joy in your presence, with eternal pleasures at your right hand. "

Psalm 31 : 20.

(20) " In the shelter of your presence you hide

20

them from the intrigues of men, in your dwelling you keep them safe from accusing tongues. "

Psalm 41 : 12.

(12) " In my integrity you uphold me and set me in your presence forever. "

Psalm 51 : 11.

(11) " Do not cast me from your presence or take your Holy Spirit from me. "

Psalm 114 : 7.

(7) " Tremble, O
earth, at the presence of
the LORD, at the presence
of the God of Jacob. "

Isaiah 26 : 17.

(17) " As a woman
with child and about to give
birth, withers and cries out
in her pain, so were we in
your presence, O LORD. "

22

John 14 : 16 - 21.

(16) " And I will ask the Father, and he will give you another Counselor to be with you forever -

(17) the Spirit of truth. The world cannot accept him, because it neither sees him nor knows him. But you know him, for he lives with you and will be in you.

(18) I will not leave you as orphans. I will come to you.

(19) Before long, the world will not see me anymore but you will see me. Because I live you also will live.

(20) On that day you will realize that i am in my Father and you are in me, and I am in you.

24

(21) Whoever has my commands and obeys them, he is the one who loves me. He who loves me will be loved by my Father, and I too will love him and show myself to him "

Hebrews 9 : 24.

(24)" For Christ did not enter a man - made sanctuary that was

only a copy of the the
true one, he entered
heaven itself, now to
appear for us in God's
presence ."

1 John 3 : 19 - 20.

(19) " This then is
how we know that we
belong to the truth, and
how we set our hearts at
rest in his presence

(20) whenever
our hearts condemn us.
For God is greater than
our hearts , and he knows
everything. "

Jude 24 - 25.

(24) To him
who is able to keep you
from falling and to
present you before his
glorious presence without
fault and with great joy -

(25) to the only

God our Saviour be glory, majesty, power and authority through Jesus Christ our Lord, before all ages, now and forevermore, " Amen ."

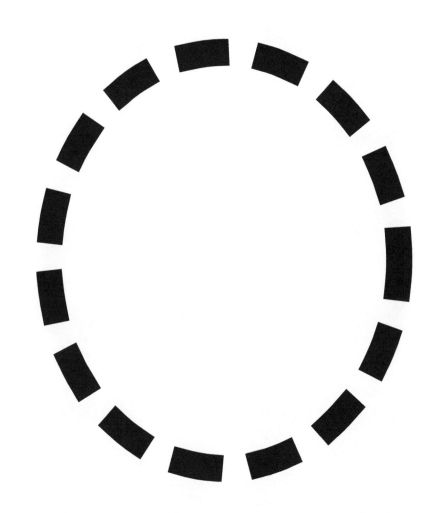

29

(C E B)

Exodus 25 : 30.

(30) " Set the bread of the presence on the table so it is always in front of me. "

Exodus 33 : 14

(14) " The LORD replied, " I'll go myself, and I'll help you. "

Numbers 4 : 7.

(7) " They will spread a blue cloth on the presentation table and place on it the plates, dishes, the bowls, and the container for the drink offering. The usual bread will be on it. "

1 Samuel 6 : 20.

(20) " The people of Beth - Shemesh said, " Who can stand before the LORD, this holy God? Where can he go that is away from us here? "

2 Kings 23 : 27.

(27) " The LORD said, " I will remove Judah from my presence

36

just as I removed Israel. I will reject this city, Jerusalem, which i chose, and this temple where I promised my name would reside. "

Psalm 16 : 11.

(11) " You teach me the way of life. In your presence is total celebration. Beautiful things are always in your right hand. "

Psalm 31 : 20.

(20) " You hide
them in the shelter of
your wings, safe from
human scheming. You
conceal them in a shelter,
safe from accusing
tongues. "

Psalm 41 : 12.

(12) " You
support me in my
integrity, you put me in

your presence forever."

Psalm 51 : 11.

(11) "Please don't
throw me out of your
presence; please don't
take your holy spirit
away from me."

Psalm 114 : 7.

(7) " Earth :
tremble before the LORD!
Tremble before the God of

Jacob, "

Isaiah 26 : 17.

(17) " As a
pregnant woman close to
childbirth is in labor
pains, crying out in her
pangs, so were we because
of you , LORD. "

John 14 : 16 - 21.

(16) " I will ask
the Father, and he will

40

send another Companion, who will be with you forever.

(17) This Companion is the Spirit of Truth, whom the world can't receive because it neither sees him nor recognizes him. You know him, because he lives with you and will be with you.

(18) I won't leave you as orphans. I will come to you.

(19) Soon the world will no longer see me, but you will see me. Because I live, you will live too.

(20) On that day you will know that i am in my father, you are in me, and I am in you.

(21) Whoever has my commandments and keeps them loves me. Whoever loves me will be loved by my Father, and I will love them and reveal myself to them."

Hebrews 9 : 24.

(24) " Christ didn't enter the holy place made by human hands (which is a copy of the true holy place) so that now he now appears in God's presence for us."

1 John 3 : 19 - 20.

(19) " This is how we will know that we belong to the truth and reassure our hearts in God's presence.

(20) Even if our hearts condemn us, God is greater than our hearts and knows all things .

44

Jude 24 - 25.

(24) " To the one
who is able to protect you
from falling, and to
present you blameless and
rejoicing before his
glorious presence.

(25) to the only
god our savior, through
Jesus Christ our Lord,
belong glory, majesty,
power, and authority,
before all time, now and
forever. Amen. "

48

49

(E S V)

Exodus 25 : 30.

(30) " And you shall set the bread of the Presence on the table before me regularly. "

Exodus 33 : 14.

(14) " And he said, " My presence will go with you, and I will give

50

you rest. "

Numbers 4 : 7.

(7) " And over the
table of the bread of the
Presence they shall
spread a cloth of blue and
put on it the plates, the
dishes for incense, the
bowls, and the flagons for
the drink offering; the
regular show bread also
shall be on it. "

1 Samuel 6 : 20.

(20) " Then the men of Beth - Shemesh said, " Who is able to stand before the LORD, this holy God? And to whom shall he go up away from us ? "

2 Kings 23 : 27.

(27) " And the LORD said, " I will

remove Judah also out of
my sight, as I have
removed Israel, and I will
cast off this city that I
have chosen, Jerusalem,
and the house of which I
said, My name shall be
there. "

Psalm 16 : 11.

(11) " You make
known to me the path of
life; in your presence
there is fullness of joy; at
your right hand are
pleasures forevermore. "

53

Psalm 31 : 20.

(20) " In the cover
of your presence you hide
them from the plots of
men; you store them in
your shelter from the
strife of tongues. "

Psalm 41 : 12.

(12) " But you
have upheld me because
of my integrity, and set
me in your presence
forever."

54

Psalm 51 : 11.

(11) " Cast me not
away from your presence,
and take not your Holy
Spirit from me. "

Psalm 114 : 7.

(7) " Tremble, O
earth, at the presence of
the Lord, at the presence
of the God of Jacob,

55

Isaiah 26 : 17.

(17) " Like a pregnant woman who writhes and cries out in her pangs when she is near to giving birth, so were we because of you, O LORD; "

John 14 : 16 - 21.

(16) " And I will
ask the Father, and he will
give you another Helper,
to be with you forever,

(17) even the
Spirit of truth, whom the
world cannot receive,
because it neither sees
him nor knows him. You
know him, for he dwells
with you and will be in
you.

(18) " I will

not leave you as orphans;
I will come to you.

(19) Yet a little
while and the world will
see me no more, but you
will see me. Because I
live, you also will live.

(20) In that
day you will know that I
am in my Father, and you
in me , and I in you.

(21) Whoever
has my commandments

58

and keeps them, he it is who loves me. And he who loves me will be loved by my Father, and I will love him and manifest myself to him. "

Hebrews 9 : 24.

(24) " For Christ has entered, not into holy places made with hands, which are copies of the true things, but into heaven itself, now to appear in the presence of

God on our behalf.

1 John 3 : 19 - 20.

(19) " By this we shall know that we are of the truth and reassure our heart before him;

(20) for whenever our heart condemns is, God is greater than our heart, and he knows everything ."

60

Jude 1 : 24 - 25.

(24) " Now to him who is able to keep you from stumbling and to present you blameless before the presence of his glory with great joy,

(25) to the only god, our Savior, through Jesus Christ our Lord, be glory, majesty, dominion, and authority, before all time and now and forever. Amen. "

62

(G N T)

Exodus 25 : 30.

(30) " The table
is to be placed in front
of the Covenant Box,
and on the table there is
always to be the sacred
bread offered to me. "

Exodus 33 : 14.

(14) " The LORD
said, " I will go with you,
and I will give you
victory. "

Numbers 4 : 7.

(7) " They shall
spread a blue cloth over
the table for the bread
offered to the LORD and
put on it the dishes, the
incense bowls, the offering

67

bowls, and the jars for the wine offering. There shall always be bread on the table. "

1 Samuel 6 : 20.

(20) " So the men of Beth Shemesh said, " Who can stand before the LORD, this holy God? Where can we send him to get him away from us? "

2 Kings 23 : 27.

(27) " The LORD
said , " I will do to Judah
what I have done to Israel:
I will banish the people of
Judah from my sight, and
I will reject Jerusalem, the
city I chose, and the
Temple, the place i said
was where I should be
worshiped. "

Psalm 16 : 11

(11) " You will
show me the path that
leads to life; your
presence fills me with joy
and brings me pleasure
forever. "

Psalm 31 : 20.

(20) " You hide
them in the safety of your
presence from the plots of
others; in a safe shelter
you hide them from the

70

insults of their enemies."

Psalm 41 : 12.

(12) " You will help me , because I do what is right; you will keep me in your presence forever."

Psalm 51 : 11.

(11) " Do not banish me from your presence ; do

not take your holy spirit
away from me. "

Psalm 114 : 7.

(7) " Tremble,
earth, at the Lord's
coming, at the presence pf
the God of Jacob, "

Isaiah 26 : 17.

(17) " You, LORD,
have made us cry out, as a

woman in labor cries out in pain. "

John 14 : 16 - 21.

(16) " I will ask the Father, and he will give you another Helper, who will stay with you forever.

(17) He is the Spirit, who reveals the truth about God. The world cannot receive him, because it cannot see him or know him. But you know him, because he remains with you and is in you.

(18) " When I go, you will not be left all alone; I will come back to you.

(19) In a little while the world will see me no more, but you will see me; and because I live, you also will live.

(20) When that day comes, you will know that i am in my Father and that you are in me, just as I am in you.

(21) " Those who accept my commandments and obey them are the ones who love me. My Father will love those who love me; I too will love them and reveal myself to them. "

Hebrews 9 : 24.

(24) " For Christ did not go into a Holy Place made by human hands, which was a copy of the real one. He went into heaven itself, where he now appears on our behalf in the presence of God. "

1 John 3 : 19 - 20.

(19) " This , then, is how we will know that we belong to the truth; this is

76

how we will be confident in God's presence.

(20) If our conscience condemns us, we know that God is greater than our conscience and that he knows everything. "

Jude 1 : 24 - 25.

(24) " To him who is able to keep you from falling and to bring you faultless and joyful before his glorious presence -

(25) to the only God our Savior, through Jesus Christ our Lord, be glory, majesty, might, and authority, from all ages past, and now, and forever and ever ! Amen. "

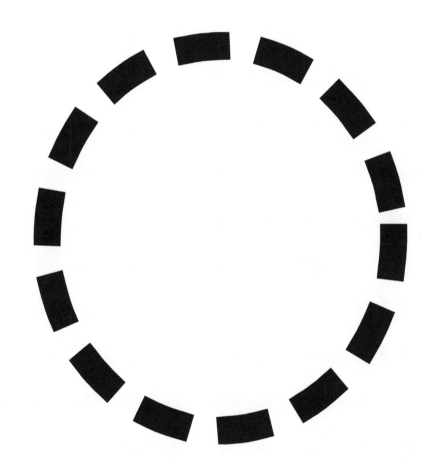

3.

The presence
of the LORD GOD
ALMIGHTY in the
Old Testament?

84

I do not intend to dwell too much on the verses cited by myself. I instead want to discuss and think about the whole idea of the presence of the LORD GOD ALMIGHTY in the Old Testament. The first thing to note about the very presence of the LORD GOD ALMIGHTY, is simply that particular individual's in the Old Testament encountered the very presence of the LORD GOD ALMIGHTY. Think about such individual's as Abram and Moses and others you can think

about for yourselves. The very
presence of the LORD GOD
ALMIGHTY was not given to all
people who believed in Him and
there was nothing they could do
to gain His very presence with
them.

Then He chooses a people
to be His own possession and His
own people and His presence is
with them as a people of the
LORD GOD ALMIGHTY. If one
considers the 40 years of
wandering in the desert by His
people; His presence was with
them and went with them , in

the tent of meeting and later in the tabernacle. The LORD GOD ALMIGHTY and His presence was with his people and yet in some ways His very presence was fixed to the tent of meeting and the specific person of Moses.

The reality, is also that the very presence of the LORD GOD ALMIGHTY could disappear if the people of the LORD GOD ALMIGHTY sinned against Him enough. Therefore, it is true that the very presence of the LORD GOD ALMIGHTY was in reality, conditional upon their own behavior before Him as His people.

As they wander in the desert we have an occasion when Moses himself says to the LORD GOD ALMIGHTY ; " *if your presence does not go with us we are not going anywhere.*"   This is in case you think that the very presence of the LORD GOD ALMIGHTY being with His people was not important to them and Moses as their leader.

We can also see this thing to do with the very presence of the LORD GOD

ALMIGHTY in the conquest of the promised land by the people of the LORD GOD ALMIGHTY. When the very presence of the LORD GOD ALMIGHTY was with them as the people of the LORD GOD ALMIGHTY; then they were victorious over those nations of people who were opposing them in their occupation of the promised land. It was like the very presence of the LORD GOD ALMIGHTY with them as a people assured them of victory over their enemies; the very nations who opposed them in the promised land.

Then fast forward to
their occupation of the promised
land and the very presence of
the LORD GOD ALMIGHTY was
with them as a people and in the
City of Jerusalem in His Temple.
The LORD GOD ALMIGHTY dwelt
amongst His people, their City
and His Temple. The Temple was
where He was supposed to dwell
in particular in the earth. Just
remember as the Temple that
King Solomon built is dedicated
to the LORD GOD ALMIGHTY, the
cloud of His presence fills the
very Temple dedicated to Him.

The City of Jerusalem was also known as the Holy City ; a City dedicated to the LORD GOD ALMIGHTY. Therefore, the LORD GOD ALMIGHTY dwelt amongst His people in the form of Israel and later Judah. But as the verses highlight He could also depart and remove His very presence from His people, His City and His Temple when they sinned against Him. This was also true of people who were filled with the presence of the LORD GOD ALMIGHTY such as King David who in Psalm 51 laments the reality that he could lose the very presence of the LORD GOD ALMIGHTY with him. Therefore ; the very presence of the LORD GOD ALMIGHTY was with particular individual's , the City, His people and His Temple and could be removed from all of them by the LORD GOD ALMIGHTY Himself; when and if they sinned against him enough, so in many ways the presence of the LORD GOD ALMIGHTY was conditional upon their behavior.

All of this became

a reality when the exile of the people of the LORD GOD ALMIGHTY happened and the City of God was conquered by the Babylonians and their King. The people had thought the very presence of the LORD GOD ALMIGHTY in their City, amongst them as the people of God and in His Temple meant that they would never be conquered and overthrown by their enemies. However, the exilic Prophets and their writings reveal that the presence of the LORD GOD ALMIGHTY was present even with His people in exile in a foreign land . One only has to read the Prophet Ezekiel to see this and understand the reality of the very presence of the LORD GOD ALMIGHTY , even with His people in their exile in Babylon.

No longer was the very presence of the LORD GOD ALMIGHTY fixed to His Temple in the City of God Jerusalem; He was in reality the LORD GOD ALMIGHTY of the whole earth and His very presence could be found and received everywhere.

After the return from exile and the rebuilding of the very Temple of the LORD GOD ALMIGHTY, the people of the LORD GOD ALMIGHTY return in many ways to the old ways of doing things. The very presence of the LORD GOD ALMIGHTY was again to be found and meditated through His dwelling upon the earth in his Temple in His City, the City of God Jerusalem . He also could be with particular people such as His Prophets . The very presence of the LORD GOD ALMIGHTY again became conditional .

96

4.

The presence of the LORD God in the New Testament .

100

Let us now turn our attention to a consideration of the very presence of the LORD God in the New Testament. In many ways the very presence of the LORD God in the New Testament centers upon the person of the Lord Jesus Christ, the very Son of God. In relation to this remember one of the names for the Lord Jesus Christ was *Emmanuel* which means God with us. Therefore, in many ways the very presence of the LORD GOD ALMIGHTY was mediated by

101

and through the Son of God, the Lord Jesus Christ. This is because not only did He have the very presence of the Father with him but also he was God Himself and also He was empowered by the third person of the trinity who was the Holy Spirit, who was God as well.

The verses cited from John 14 : 16 - 21 are interesting and inform us that after the Lord Jesus Christ has ascended back to the Father He will leave the Holy Spirit to be with His follower's.

So therefore ; the very presence of the LORD GOD ALMIGHTY comes to us as believer's in the Lord Jesus Christ through the mediation of the Holy Spirit ; who is also the LORD GOD ALMIGHTY as well, the third person of the trinity God Himself. No longer is the very presence of the LORD GOD ALMIGHTY conditional upon our behavior rather the third person the trinity , the Holy Spirit is given as a free gift and He will never depart from us . This is in stark contrast to the

Old Testament where the presence of the LORD GOD ALMIGHTY was dependent upon the behavior of the people and the person. The presence of the LORD GOD ALMIGHTY could depart if there was sin and wrongdoing in the people's lives and in the individual's life as well.

In some ways , that is why we post - cross are part of the New Covenant. The very presence of the LORD GOD ALMIGHTY; through the third person of the trinity, the Holy

Spirit remains with the believer's in the Lord Jesus Christ. He is given as a free gift when a person comes to faith in the Lord Jesus Christ. His presence is also the very guarantee that the person will receive the gift of eternal life when they die in their faith in the Lord Jesus Christ. So therefore; not only does the presence of the Holy Spirit bring the very presence of the LORD GOD ALMIGHTY but also He is the deposit in terms of eternal life and it's reception by the believer in the Lord Jesus Christ.

No longer does one have to go to the Temple of the LORD GOD ALMIGHTY to be in His very presence; instead we as believer's carry the very presence of the LORD GOD ALMIGHTY with us wherever we are. All of which is why the Apostle Paul could rightly talk about the believer in the Lord Jesus Christ being a temple of the Holy Spirit. I believe behind this imagery from the Apostle Paul was the very reality that when a believer comes to faith in the Lord Jesus Christ they receive the Holy Spirit; to live and reside within

106

them. So, in many ways one could really see how believer's in the Lord Jesus Christ could be aptly called temples of the Holy Spirit.

In the verses cited from the New Testament; there is also a sense of the Lord Jesus Christ now that He has ascended back to the Father and heaven being in the very presence of His Father and representing us to His Father. The technical theological term for all of this ; is that, *the Lord Jesus Christ is in session at the right hand of the*

Father. So therefore, there is also this sense of the very presence of the Father, the LORD GOD ALMIGHTY that has to be factored into the discussion of the presence of the LORD GOD ALMIGHTY in the New Testament. There is also a sense in which the believer in the Lord Jesus Christ, themselves has access to the very presence of the Father , through the Son of God, the Lord Jesus Christ. The Letter to the Hebrews tells us this graphically and says some thing like *we can come boldly before the very throne of grace through the Son of God, the Lord Jesus Christ.*

108

So from all of this one can see that post - cross there really is a whole New Covenant and ways and means of receiving the very presence of the LORD GOD ALMIGHTY. The Lord Jesus Christ said that " He would never leave or forsake those who were His." The ways and means of this promise , is that, through having the Holy Spirit within us as believer's we always have the very presence of the LORD GOD ALMIGHTY within us as believer's in the Lord Jesus Christ; the Son of God.

All of which is why it is so

important to come to faith in the Lord Jesus Christ as a believer in Him. When one does this they receive the free gift of the very presence of the LORD GOD ALMIGHTY within themselves; in the form of the third person of the trinity , the Holy Spirit. It's interesting to note that in John 14 the Holy Spirit, is also referred to by the Lord Jesus Christ as the Spirit of Truth. So, if you want to receive truth, the very truth about the Son of God, the Lord Jesus Christ , then one needs to receive the gift of the Holy Spirit by coming to belief in the Lord Jesus Christ.

110

All of which is why the Lord Jesus Christ Himself saw it as very important that His follower's received the Holy Spirit, the very presence of the LORD GOD ALMIGHTY living within them personally. The Holy Spirit empowers the believer to witness and testify to the Lord Jesus Christ and the truth about Him. The follower's in the Lord Jesus Christ, the Son of God could not hope to survive without the presence of the Holy Spirit within them.

114

5.

EPILOGUE :

Within this very book; an attempt has been made to

trace throughout
the Word of God
the notion of the
presence of the
LORD GOD
ALMIGHTY. What
the very presence
of the LORD GOD
ALMIGHTY
looked like in the
Old Testament

was discussed with broad brush strokes. It was seen how the very presence of the LORD GOD ALMIGHTY was largely dependent upon the behavior of the people of God and the individual being used by the LORD GOD ALMIGHTY for a specific purpose and time. The very presence of the LORD GOD ALMIGHTY could depart from the people, the person and even the City of God, Jerusalem. Therefore, there was no guarantee regarding having the very presence of the LORD GOD ALMIGHTY with you as a people, person or the City of God. The very

presence of the
LORD GOD
ALMIGHTY could
be removed by
Him when he felt
like it and when
the wrongdoing
and sin of the
people, land and
City of God was
too much for Him.

Fast forward
to the New
Testament and
the New Covenant
in the very blood
of the Lord Jesus
Christ, the very
Son of God and
there is a new
deal regards the
very presence of

122

the LORD GOD ALMIGHTY. After the Lord Jesus Christ, the very Son of God ascends back to the Father and heaven he leaves with His followers the gift of the Holy Spirit. He is both the guarantee of the presence of the LORD GOD ALMIGHTY within a believer's life, as well as being the very Spirit of Truth. He is the one who leads the person into all the truth about the Lord Jesus Christ, His life, death and resurrection from the dead.

So now post - cross the believer's in the Lord Jesus Christ have the very presence of the LORD GOD ALMIGHTY within themselves. No longer is the LORD GOD ALMIGHTY distant and removed from those who believe

126

in Him. The believer is in fact the very temple of the Holy Spirit; as per the Apostle Paul's description of believer's in the letter to the Corinthians.

THE AUTHOR :

JOHN C BURT.

132

JOHN WORSHIPS AT ST. PHILLIPS, ANGLICAN CHURCH, AUBURN, NSW, AUSTRALIA. IT IS A LIVELY, MULTI - CULTURAL CONGREGATION AND CHURCH.

JOHN ENJOYS THE ODD CUP OF COFFEE, BUT IT HAS TO BE HOT AS HOT AND FROTHY. JOHN SOMETIMES FREQUENTS THE CAFES IN AUBURN AREA.

134

JOHN ALSO ENJOYS CHICKEN AND JELLYFISH; A CHINESE DISH WHICH IS USUALLY SERVED COLD. JOHN ALSO ENJOYS OCCASIONALLY PIZZA AS WELL.

AMEN

AND

AMEN...

MAY THE
PEACE OF
THE LORD
JESUS CHRIST
RULE IN
YOUR HEART
AND MINDS.
AMEN ...

140

141

Lightning Source UK Ltd.
Milton Keynes UK
UKHW020347091019
351227UK00001B/8/P

9 780368 254147